THE FOUR SEASONS

EVERY SEASON HAS ITS BEGINNING

BY
PATRICIA A. FLORIO

THE FOUR SEASONS

Copyright © 2024 Patricia A. Florio

All rights reserved. No part of this book may be reproduced, distributed, or transmitted in any form or by any means, including photocopying, recording, or other electronic or mechanical methods, without the prior written permission of the author, except in the case of brief quotations embodied in critical reviews and certain other non-commercial uses permitted by copyright law. For permission requests, please contact the author.

Publisher Information

America Publishers
Email: info@americapublishers.com
Phone: +1 (617) 334-5774

ISBN Information

eBook: 978-1-966198-23-9
Paperback: 978-1-966198-24-6
Hardcover: 978-1-966198-25-3

Cover Design by: America Publishers

Printed in the United States of America

1st Edition: November, 2024

THE FOUR SEASONS

EVERY SEASON HAS ITS BEGINNING

Dedication

This book is dedicated to the people of Ocean Grove, New Jersey, especially Doctor Arlene Cardinale and John MacAllister's presence in our lives was second to none.

They were our friends. They are still our friends, no matter where life or death has taken them.

I see these people in my dreams; they have meant and still mean so much to me. We meant a lot to one another. Never let it be said, like when the Towers fell in on 9-11 in New York City: we will never forget you. Never! We will never forget the two of you; you were our friends and will always be our friends.

I hope I am not being redundant. These people were human beings. They understood the principle of life: Love one another, as I have loved you.

Table of Contents

Dedication i

Chapter 1: Our lives in movement 1

Chapter 2: Meeting people for the first time 5

Chapter 3: The Retirement House 9

Chapter 4: The Beach Community 19

Spring 34

Fall 39

Winter 46

Summer 54

Finale 59

A Tribute to 62

Meet the Author 65

A Personal Note from Patricia A. Florio 66

About the Author 68

About the Book 70

About the Publisher 72

Chapter 1:

Our lives in movement

On Thursday, 1998, three days before New Year's Eve, my husband and I packed up our house in Manalapan, NJ, to move to our new retirement home in Ocean Grove. It was cold outside, and we packed furiously – boxes were everywhere.

My daughter Kristin was miserable. She didn't want to move, but she had no choice. We were her parents, and she had to come live with us. I knew she would miss

Shaun and Nancy, with whom she had gone to junior high and high school.

As the movers put the boxes in the truck, Kristin packed her red Firebird with stuffed animals. The big stuffed bear sat in the passenger seat next to her. The fluffy tiger, its head was plopped over her head in the driver's seat. She had a dozen cabbage patch dolls sitting in the back seat. There were stuffed animals of every variety, shape, and color.

I smelled snow in the air. Snow has a distinct smell: Fresh, icy, tingly on my fingertips. I love snow. Well, the first day anyway. The rest is a big mess, with parked cars everywhere, and ice cycles dangling from street wires.

I'm always afraid a transmission cable might go out and we would be stuck without lights.

I love writing and was working on an essay for school, about *Old Statements that Aren't Famous*: Like don't get old!

Who says, that? Well, my Aunt Jennie does. She didn't die until she was ninety-nine years old. My mother would have been pissed at her sister because she passed away at ninety-five. My mother and her sister, Jennie, were always in great competitions, even when they were old.

A few months before we moved into our retirement home, we drove to Ocean Grove and took along some friends. Stu and Helen were interested in what kind of a house we were buying to retire in. I had always loved the beach. Since I was six years old, I had been going to the beach with my parents. We always via the F train to Coney Island.

One day, I told my husband Ralph, "I never want to car it or train it or plane it to the beach. I want to walk."

Chapter 2:

Meeting people for the first time

When we got to Ocean Grove, we pulled up to our new house. It was October. The sun was warm. Two women were sitting in the front yard of the house next door to the one we had purchased.

"Are you the new owners?" the tall blonde woman asked.

I said, "Yes, we are Ralph and Pat Florio." These are our friends Helen and Stuart. Helen had been my friend for several years. She had helped me many years earlier escape out of my house unscathed with my twin boys when I was getting divorced from their father.

Helen also had a baby back then. But she gave it up for adoption. She had had this baby girl out of wedlock, something that Stu didn't know about. I wasn't going to tell him. But I noticed Helen looking at the pregnant woman sitting in the blue lawn chair.

Diane walked out from the white front gate and said, "This is my partner, Karen. She's having twins."

It was obvious. Karen was huge. I had had twins myself twenty-something years ago. Anthony and Joseph were my sons from my first marriage. Ralph adopted them when their father didn't come forward.

My lawyer had us post an ad in several local newspapers to announce that if he, the father, didn't come forward, they would be adopted by Ralph F. Florio.

My sister-in-law Terry, my brother's wife, used to say, "I can see your belly, Pat, long before you turn the corner." Ha! That's how big I was when I was pregnant, and that's exactly how big Karen was, too.

Terry is now deceased but comes to me as a muse some nights and says I should get out of bed and write.

Of course, I listen to her. She is a great muse. I write everything she tells me to write. Most things are about her husband, my brother, Joe, because he was such a good man.

I am now looking at Karen and I know from my own experience of having twins, what she is in for; what these two women are both in for, having had a set of twins was no walk in the park.

My brother used to say, "Pat, you should have been born with four arms and four hands."

I guess that's true!

Ralph and I fell in love with Karen and Diane from the first minute we met.

We are like that. We love people and people love us.

Chapter 3:

The Retirement House

This new house was the third house from the beach; in the same place as our Manalapan home, where we were the third house from the corner, where the first house had a set of twin girls, and the fourth house, next door to us, had triplets. We were destined to fill the world with children: They are our future.

That Manalapan house is a five-bedroom colonial with a brick walkway with beautiful white columns. We planted a pine tree on the right-hand side of the house and decorated it every Christmas.

I had read a magazine article years earlier about Governor Mario Cuomo who did the same thing in front of his New York home. Only, the governor buried treasures under his Christmas tree so that when aliens came from outer space, they would understand our species.

I buried some kitchen utensils and a statue of Saint Joseph, the patron saint of selling homes.

Thank you, Saint Joseph, for helping us sell our house.

We went to closing two days before New Year's Eve. We had plans to spend the Eve with Louie and Joyce

Burdo, friends from Brooklyn. We knew Louie and Joyce and their daughter Nicole for many years. Nicole and Kristin went to Manalapan High School together.

After our dinner in Atlantic City, where we partied hardy, we went back to Cape May to sleep.

The next day, New Year's day, as usual, we went to my mother's house in downtown Brooklyn for dinner. The usual suspects were there. My aunts and uncles, cousins, kids. The table was filled with wine, beer, pasta, Sunday sauce, and meat.

My mother prepared a loin of pork, a delicious cut of meat, with apple sauce, which is one of Ralph's favorites.

Ralph was working for the district attorney's office in Brooklyn on New Year's Day, and he was on call.

Right about 4 o'clock, Ralph got a phone call to meet a homicide detective at the 92nd Precinct in Canarsie, Brooklyn, to take a statement on his court reporting machine.

My kids were thrilled. They wanted to see the inside of the precinct, a jail cell, and the keys that opened and locked the prisoners inside.

Off we went.

Since, I had been Ralph's transcriber, whatever statement he took down on his steno machine, I typed up for the ADA who was in charge of the case.

Mr. Bob Russell was Ralph's supervisor. At that time in 1998, we didn't know this, but Bob and I would go into business together one day.

A year later, we solidified our agreement and started a freelance-reporting agency called *All Borough Reporting*.

Our female stenographers, the freelancers: Margie, Mary, Yolanda, and Holly were the cream of the crop. But also prima donnas. They weren't happy if they couldn't see the job from the window. That was said as a joke, but it was true. These girls were fussy about taking trains to the Bronx. I couldn't blame them, but we were called *All Borough*.

I also went to school in those days. Call me an overachiever. I took the entrance exam for Brookdale Community College. That's where I met Carol MacAllister. Carol lived in the first house on the second beach block on my block, Embury Avenue, with her husband John.

John and Carol were licensed electricians. They owned Breaker Electric. Carol and I were in the same creative writing class. Gene Schneider was our professor. I wrote a lot in those days. I still write a lot. I remember the first letter I ever wrote. I was six years old sitting under my grandmother's fig tree in the house's backyard where we lived in Brooklyn.

I wrote to my brother Joe. He was ten years older me. Joe was in the Air Force stationed in the Azores during the Korean conflict.

My brother was there on a secret mission and when his letters hit the States, they were censored and closed with a big piece of brown tape.

For Gene's class, I wrote *The Biggest Bet of All*. It was about my girlfriend Margaret, her cousin Ester, and Smash. Her real name was Eleanor. We called her Smash because she has a nose like a prize fighter.

Those were the good old days in our Italian ghetto when you smelled meatballs frying every Sunday morning, where the women hung their clothes out on the line to dry. Where we felt safe and comfortable in our homes every night. I loved being a kid in Brooklyn. I loved being a tomboy. I jumped over the gaps of the brownstones' roofs. We gained access to these black tar roofs through Marguerite's bathroom skylight. There was a steel ladder and up we would climb and then crawl on our bellies so no one from the street would see us. We were bad girls, but not the way you might be thinking. We didn't have sex with boys. Heck, we didn't even kiss boys. But that would change a few years later. Yep, it takes a few years and everything changes, even me.

Now, I'm in high school. Oh boy, the nuns picked me out to go on a vocational retreat to be a nun. I didn't want to be a nun. I had a boyfriend at the time, but off I went, always listening to Sister Mary Peter and I traveled by train upstate to Mount Kisco, where we got up at four in the morning to pray for the world.

You know, I still do that sometimes, pray for the world.

I didn't become a nun, and I didn't want to get married, but my father made me get married. He wanted me out of his hair, just like he wanted my brother Joe. That's why my brother joined the Air Force, to get out from under my father's reign.

My father didn't believe in higher education for women. He was an old-fashioned Italian laborer who worked at the piers at the Brooklyn Army Base.

He believed all women should get married and have babies. Oh, shit, I'm getting off the subject. My mind wanders a lot. Let me get back to Ocean Grove and my friend Carol.

Rich DeMartin worked for John and Carol at Breaker Electric. John MacAllister was his boss. Rich is a nice man. He has dark hair, although I think he colors it to get rid of the grays ones now coming in. He's married to Annie. Their house is right behind mine on Webb Avenue.

I met Rich one day outside Carol's house. I was there admiring the flowers that grew so hardy in the front of her garden. Carol always planted beautiful flowers that bloomed like a forest. The ones that smelled like perfume. Pink roses, red roses. Lilacs and climbing ivy. She had a Victorian Home, one of the best in Ocean Grove.

Chapter 4:

The Beach Community

Our town by the sea is a lot like Cape May. It's a Historic Victorian town with gingerbread houses, turrets, and beautiful color paint on the facade. Ocean Grove looks like a box of crayons. The box with all the colors, not just the primary ones.

During those days, Rich and Annie owned a laundromat that spanned from one block to the other: from Maine Avenue to the following block, with another door out into the parking lot, where the customers picked up their wash and fold.

We always worked long hours and it was a great idea to drop our clothes off in the morning, and have Cheryl, who worked there, oversee that part of the business.

Cheryl worked for Rich. She has cropped blonde hair, and she has a granddaughter who went to school with my granddaughter Amelia. These kids, Amelia and Cheryl's granddaughter, Mia, are talented. Amelia sings. She knocks the socks off the audience at her school in Bradley Beach.

Annie, Rich's wife, also sells jewelry outside the store on Saturdays. Our downtown Maine Avenue has several boutiques and fine eateries. Moonstruck is our favorite restaurant. This is an upscale place. Luke and Howard own it, and named it for the movie with Cher and Nick Cage.

Luke's grandparents and mine came from the same town in Naples, Italy (Prato La Sera). The dinners who eat there are allowed to bring wine and other spirits. Ocean Grove is a dry town. It's a Camp Meeting Town started by the Methodists in 1869, as a town for rest and restoration. It does not have liquor licenses, so all the restaurants are BYOB (bring your own booze.)

Carol MacAllister knew everyone in town, as the town electrician. She introduced Ralph and me to Leonard and Arlene who lived diagonal from her house on Embury Avenue. We are right up the street from Carol and John. They see us from their bedroom window when we come home late from work.

Len and Arlene are Italians from Newark. We are Italians from Brooklyn, so Carol figured we'd have alot in common.

Do you know what happens when Italians from Brooklyn meet Italians from Newark? Sparks fly and kisses are placed on both cheeks. And we begin to sing Dean Martin songs.

Both Len and Arlene were principals of schools. Leonard was the principal of a boy's high school. I think the name was Barringer. Arlene was the principal of the grammar school. The one she went to when she was a child.

I found this out when I did a profile piece about Arlene for a weekly Red Bank newspaper owned by Geraldo Rivera. *The Two River Times* ran the article: *From School Books to Fishing Hooks*. Arlene had become the first woman president of Ocean Grove Fishing Club in over one hundred years.

Arlene was a beautiful woman. She had blond hair and wore just the right clothes. I remember her telling me she modeled hats as a young girl. She always looked like a million dollars. Leonard did too! He's the professor type, gray beard, fine suits, and a swagger to his step. They always smelled good. They both used Jean Natae, a bath liquid. Its aroma was heavenly.

So here we are four couples who live in Ocean Grove who had arranged to have dinner together one night. We all packed our BYOB and met at a restaurant near Long Branch, somewhere around Monmouth Beach.

But I'm not ready yet to let you in on the secrets these couples shared. But we will talk about that soon.

IN THE PAST:

Louie and Joyce's daughter Michelle, her godfather was named Lenny. I had dated Lenny for two years before I met Ralph. He was a nice guy, but I was much older than him. When he took me to meet his parents, his mother said to me, "This is not the way I thought I would meet my future daughter-in-law: A divorced woman with two kids."

Lenny didn't seem to mind, although he wasn't a nice guy to my kids. He always wanted to jump in the sack. And that wasn't possible with my children around. I was starting to get fed up with Lenny. That's exactly the day Ralph Florio, my husband of fifty-three years now, walked into the bowling alley.

Tony Campanella, one of the owners of Leader Lanes introduced me to Ralph, as I worked behind the desk. I rented shoes to bowlers and gave them their score sheets.

Tony informed me that Ralph had just come home from Vietnam and that I shouldn't charge Ralph for bowling because he was a professional bowler and would give free lessons to the women and men who came in to bowl.

I was happy with that arrangement. When Ralph came in to bowl his practice games, I handed him a score sheet, and off he went to Lane 25, an odd lane in the house, where no one would bother him.

Ralph practiced two or three hours a day. Then when he finished practicing, he sat at the snack bar and had a cup of coffee.

He walked over to the desk to hand back the score sheet and asked me, "Are you married to Tony Campanella?"

"No, I said. I'm a single mom. Those two boys you see coming in every afternoon. That's Anthony and Joseph, my twin sons."

From that day forward, when the boys came in for lunch or after school, they sat with Ralph at the snack bar.

One day, out of the blue, Ralph asked if he could take the boys out for ice cream. I looked at these kids. Their eyes were begging me to say yes. "Okay," I said. I wasn't afraid Ralph would steal them. I trusted him.

When they came back, they were all smiles, with chocolate all over their shirts.

"I hope you're not angry," Ralph said.

I wasn't angry. I was happy for my boys. I was happy they had a nice man paying attention to them.

The next afternoon, Ralph took my sons to his home to meet his mother Mary and his father Big Ralph.

My boys were thrilled! They came back telling stories about Gina, Big Ralph's dog. Gina was a German shepherd. They loved her. I was starting to fall for this guy with the pleasant smile and chipped tooth. Who was he and what did he want with my children?

I won't say Lenny couldn't stand my children, but he wasn't nice to them.

It was August 3, 1971, and I worked the night shift at the bar. I needed the money, and I took the waitress job. The lounge is where Ralph and I danced to the Flamingos' song, *I only have eyes for you*. The Flamingos and Chicago were Ralph's favorite groups.

Mary and Ralph were going to the racetrack one night and they asked Ralph and me to come with them. I wanted to go, but my mother was pestering me about Lenny. She didn't understand that his parents hated me. How could I tell her that?

Anyway, Lenny comes to the bowling alley and asks me to go outside with him. Ralph follows. "You said you'd go out with me for my birthday." Lenny grabbed me by the wrist. Ralph went crazy. He punched the living shit out of Lenny. But Lenny, that little creep, went back to my house and told my mother, showing her his black eye.

My mother went wild. She had broken her foot about a month earlier, running away from a squirrel in our garage. She came out with a broom and told Ralph, "Get out of here, you hoodlum, stay away from my daughter."

Ralph called my phone from the phone booth on the corner of East 2nd Street where I lived. "Is your mother crazy?" he asked.

Yes, I said, "My mother is as crazy as a loon. But she will get over it."

That Christmas Eve at Mary and Big Ralph's, Ralph left a box on my dinner plate.

"What's this," I asked, "for me?"

"Open it, Mom," said Anthony in his Alvin the Chipmunk voice. "Open it," Joseph chimed in too.

Inside the box was an engagement ring. It wasn't a diamond. It was an opal – my birthstone. Ralph was proposing to me. I couldn't have been happier. I was 28 years old. Ralph was 30 and we were so excited to have found one another. Love like this doesn't happen every day. You must grab onto it with everything you have, and never let it go. I was never going to let Ralph go. I had found my soulmate. Happiness oozed from every pore of my body.

My mother was finally happy to see her daughter at peace and in love. She asked one thing of us: to get married in church.

We promised we would not disappoint her. It was a great Christmas Eve and a wonderful and blessed New Year.

Spring

I think of Annie and Rich as Spring because they both have birthdays in Spring. Rich's birthday is in April and Annie's is in May. They are the spring couple of our group. We are, all four couples, in this Italian restaurant. We have red wine, white wine, and Marie Bizzard. Marie is a favorite drink of Italians, especially in black coffee. Italian black coffee. It's strong. It will knock your socks off. It's an after-dinner coffee, great with a cannoli. We think that's what we will have for dessert, but we haven't even started dinner and we're thinking of cake and coffee. We are all good eaters. *Magange bene! Bona fortuna!*

Annie is a talker. She loves expressing herself, and she starts off the conversation. "You know," she says, "I met Richard at *Parents Without Partners*. I was lonely after my divorce, and I wanted to find a person who I could converse with. I have a daughter Christie. She's a beautiful little girl, with no brothers or sisters. I have a brother, but he's not well. I was lonely. I took a chance this one night that maybe tonight was the night that I would meet someone." Richard was standing talking to a few men and I took a chance, I walked over, and I introduced myself. "I am Anne."

Richard says, "I'm Richard. Would you like a cup of coffee? They are just bringing it out fresh."

I accepted Rich's offer for coffee, and we started to talk about our families. Richard mentioned his ex-wife was not a well woman in the head. He had two adult children. I liked him right from the beginning. We dated for a while, and I was kind of scared that he wasn't going to ask me to get married. I was brave. I asked him. I said, "Richard, I'm alone with Christie. My mother left me all this money. Why don't we buy a house at the shore? They are building some new ones. I had researched Ocean Grove, and it looked like a small little town where Richard and I could be happy. So, I bought 3 Webb Avenue, and we moved in together with Christie. But the schools are not the best in Neptune. Richard had this idea about opening a laundry. The town only had one and it was starting to grow. That October, we got married, and moved into a house in little community called Colts Neck, and decided to rent the beach house, but with an apartment in the back for us to use when we came to the shore."

Carol says, "Anne and Richard were smart not to put their apples in one basket. They branched out and it paid off for them. They have an income coming in during the summer months. The laundry is a success. Not like John and me at all. We were flat broke when we got together."

Fall

Carol and John are my fall couple. I know fall doesn't follow spring, so don't think I'm making a mistake. It will all become clear. I promise you.

Carol starts the conversation. "John is not a talker. He's more anti-social than social." But John Mac, as we called him, was a generous man. You needed electric? John and Carol were there with a toolbox in hand. They were the kindest and most generous of couples. Ralph and I were the party couple. We have gotten John and Carol so drunk at our house that Carol mentioned one night walking home, which is only a hundred steps away from our house, they couldn't walk. They stumbled all the way home. Carol said that night, she and John slept underneath the mattress cover they were so blitzed.

Carol says, "You know John and I were high school sweethearts. I've known John since I am fourteen years old."

I had known this story, but Len and Arlene didn't know anything about their neighbors and they were all ears.

Carol continues: "My mother thought John wasn't good enough for me. She called him a Greaser because he came to my house in an undershirt with a pack of cigarettes rolled up in his sleeve. You know like the Fonzie from Happy Days."

We are all attentive to Carol. She is an intelligent woman. She has had a great education and was an art teacher at Upper Freehold High School. I loved Carol. She was a good friend. But she never came out of the house, and I was lonely for a friend. Carol wrote all day, or she painted. Occasionally, we'd go to the beach. She'd take me far out into the ocean, and we'd jump waves together. I really liked Carol.

Today in 2024, we are separated by miles. She's in Denver, Colorado and I'm in Palm Beach, Florida. But we have Messenger, Facebook, texts, and pictures. Carol is nine months older than I am. We're getting on in age, but it was good that night when the eight of us came to know each other intimately.

Carol continues. "Once John was in the Army, my mother introduced me to this man who owned a big business. Formica. I wrote John a *Dear John letter*. I cried myself to sleep. Within the next five months, I was engaged to be married. My mother was happy, but I wasn't. I became this man's hostess to his clientele. I had two boys, Jeffrey and Tucker, and for the next thirteen or fourteen years, I was a wife and mother. But I couldn't get John out of my head. I got up with enough courage, and called a cousin of his, and I asked where he was. His cousin gave me his phone number. John had been married three times. He was as unhappy as I was. He also owned a theater playhouse in New Jersey and an electric company with his brother. I confessed to my husband that I was going back to John. I hadn't seen him in thirteen years but I didn't care." My heart said: Do it. Go find the love of your life. My husband took me and the boys to Chicago O'Hare Airport and John was there waiting for me. He handed me over to John and said, "Take her. She never loved me."

John gave him a dirty look, "You took my girlfriend away from me." Before a fight broke out, I grabbed John, the boys followed and we made our way to the ticket counter, and we bought tickets to fly back to New Jersey. John and I worked day and night. He taught me how to pull wire and we worked nights after our day jobs. We bought a tiny house until we could afford a condo in Brielle, New Jersey.

Then I sit next to this one (she's pointing at me) in a creative writing class.

I have tears running down my face. "I love her. She loves me. We are neighbors."

Winter

Ralph and I are winter. I decided to call us winter: because we got married on January 21, 1972, in Las Vegas on the Professional Bowlers' Tour. We had only been engaged six weeks. If this wasn't love, then I don't know what love is. My mother allowed me – gave me her permission – a 28-year-old woman – her blessing to visit Ralph as he bowled in Las Vegas.

I'll start my story.

"I'm sitting on a plane heading to Las Vegas. This was the first time in six years I left my boys at my brother's house on Long Island. I was nervous, well, jittery. Because of the plane, the time of day, late in the evening, and as we fly West, the daylight starts streaming into the windows. I'm heading into the sunlight. That's a good sign. My day is brighter the closer we get to Nevada. I'm on the plane with John and Linda. They are Ralph's sponsors on the professional bowler's tour. They paid for my plane ticket. I couldn't afford it. They are rich. They own a plumbing company in Brooklyn. I have about a hundred dollars to my name. I had been on social services since my divorce from my first husband."

As the plane lands, I am sweating with anticipation. I can smell my own perspiration. It's musky and I feel dirty. I run into the plane's bathroom and brush my teeth. At least that I can do. We land and taxi into the plane's parking spot. I think of the plane as a car. I don't know what to think is going to happen when I get off this plane and see Ralph. I look for him as I walk down the steps. He's there. He has a big smile on his face, and his chipped tooth is evident. He grabs me up in his arms. I feel safe all over. He kisses me, and says, "We are getting married this week. It's all arranged."

I don't say anything. I can't speak. I think of my mother. She will kill me. I know her. She's fierce. She wants me married in church before God.

"I can't," I whisper in his ear.

"Why can't you, Pat? You are a grown woman with two children."

"My mother. She will kill me."

"Pat, you are twenty-eight years old." I am twenty-eight years old. My stomach rumbles. "Promise you'll think about it."

"Okay, Ralph, I'll think about it."

We get to the hotel where the bowling alley is inside, where the bowlers are practicing, getting ready for the next day that the tournament starts.

I met up with the bowlers that I already knew from my job as the desk clerk of Leader Lanes. I'm thinking about what I should do about getting married. John and Linda are in on this. They set up the arrangements at the Chapel of the Bells.

Ralph throws his roommate, Ralph Hartman, out of the room with two beds, and says to him, "Ralph, I'm sorry, Pat is here and she's staying in the room with me. You'll have to bunk with someone else."

Ralph Hartman is a good friend. He understands. Ralph H. I'll call him so we are not confused. Two Ralphs. I mean this is crazy. I never knew one Ralph. Now, I know three: Big Ralph, my Ralph, and now Ralph H.

After dinner, I say to my Ralph, "I can't do it."

I'm weeping like a crazy woman. "I can't marry you this week."

Ralph is sad. I understand his sadness. Why am I so afraid of my mother? She isn't a bad person; she's just demanding. But my sons, Anthony and Joseph would be so happy.

"I promise, Ralph, I'm going to pray over this. Please give me tonight. Let me sleep on it. We are now in separate beds. I can hear Ralph's frustration under the covers."

The next morning when I awake, Ralph is not there. He is already bowling in the tournament. "Jesus," I pray, "this is a good man. Please help me."

We go out to dinner that night with John and Linda. They had already canceled the Chapel of the Bells. The wedding was postponed or off the table. I toast the New Year that has just passed, and I look at Ralph's face. He is sad. I hate it when he's sad. There's no smile.

"Okay," I say, "I'll do it."

Friday, January 21, 1972, we go to the Chapel of the Bells. We are filling out the marriage license paperwork. I am filling out my half, and I notice Ralph, as he is completing his half. I see him write his birthday as November 18, 1947.

I am shocked. I was born in 1943. He lied to me. He's not thirty years old. He's twenty-five. Oh my God, I think. We are starting this marriage off with a lie.

By this time, at the restaurant in Monmouth Beach, everybody has drunk a lot of wine and Marie Bizzard. We are all laughing and crying. We are having a great time.

Summer

Arlene and Leonard are Summer in my mind. I say this because summer in Ocean Grove is a special time of year. It is beach weather. People are fishing off the pier at the end of Embury Avenue. It's when we all sit outdoors, eat, drink, talk, let the kids run around, ride bikes, and jog, We just live to enjoy the community we are surrounded by.

Friday night is very special in Ocean Grove. It's the start of the weekend, and the porch lights go on, and people are sitting on their rocking chairs.

I noticed Arlene's waiting to share their life story. She starts. Leonard is smiling. He's going to allow her to introduce their secret life story. Arlene says, "So you think you have stories? Well, Leonard and I have been together for thirty-two years and we're not married yet!"

"What," I say, "You're living in sin?"

Leonard, he's so cute, with his PHD look, the ultimate professor.

He chuckles. "We met on a picket line. We were on strike. Teachers on Strike."

I look over at Arlene. She's smiling: "Just like all of you, we knew we were meant to be together. But because we worked in the same district of Newark, it's frowned upon to be married. So, we never got married."

Leonard chimes in, "Arlene had her house. I had mine, and eventually, we bought one here in Ocean Grove and have lived together as husband and wife ever since. She is still Arlene Cardinale and will always be Arlene Cardinale. I'm Dr. Leonard Pugliese. There's nothing wrong with that as far as I can see. Don't you agree?"

Leonard is looking right at me, the Holy Roller of the group.

I interject, "I'm doing a profile piece on Arlene for the newspaper, what do I say, he's your significant other, or boyfriend, husband, what do I call Leonard?"

"I'll tell you when we come back from our seminar next week."

I had time. I wrote profiles every month. It didn't matter when I put Arlene's in. Geraldo was good about that. Eileen Moon was my editor, and she loved my writing, and the stories I presented to the weekly newspaper, so I wasn't worried.

We left the restaurant a bit happier, having known one another more intimately. We were good friends. We will always be good friends. We had belly laughs to the point of almost throwing up. We found one another so funny. I loved this town. I loved my life. I loved my friends. I loved my husband. I was a lucky woman and I still am.

About a week after our dinner out in Monmouth Beach, I got a phone call from Arlene, "Hey, Pat, you know that profile piece?"

"Yes," I answered, "What about it?"

"Well, you can tell the world that Leonard is my husband. We got married while we were at the seminar."

"OMG! Arlene and Leonard are married." I yell into the kitchen for Ralph, "Get on the phone, and listen to Mrs. Pugliese."

"Wait, wait," Arlene says, "No Pugliese, I'm still Arlene Cardinale. And that's the way it's going to stay."

FINALE

Arlene Cardinale and John MacAllister left us for a greater place in the universe. We miss them. They were part of our lives for a long time, and we are still attached to their spirit. They glow out there somewhere in the universe. They always will if I have anything to say about it.

That's where I should end our stories, but something happened to me in church this morning that I'd like to share with you.

After the reading of the gospel of Luke about John the Baptist, the priest broke down the reading in this way.

"What's the difference between happiness and joy?"

I listened intently because I had always known from my Marriage Encounter days in the Church that feelings weren't right or wrong; they just are emotions.

Being happy is a fleeting emotion. It comes and it goes. But joy, joy is a more substantial emotion. Like John the Baptist. He knew internally that there would be One Greater than Him. This filled John with Joy.

I understand Joy now. I'm in that state of Joy maybe for the first time in my life. I am filled with the Spirit of the Lord, and this, my friends, is Joy.

Seek out good friends. You will know them when you find them. And perhaps like all of us, you found them already.

Go with your gut. It will never lie to you. Be joyful, be a good friend, find people whom you can love, and stick close to them all the days of your life.

END

Patricia A. Florio

A Tribute to

The Four Seasons

John MacAllister

John generously applied his electrical expertise to the Cape Meeting Association, offering his services free of charge.

Patricia A. Florio

ARLENE A. CARDINALE

FIRST WOMAN PRESIDENT OF THE OCEAN GROVE FISHING CLUB

MEET THE AUTHOR

PATRICIA A. FLORIO

A Personal Note from Patricia A. Florio

Dear Reader,

Thank you for taking the time to experience *The Four Seasons*. This book is a reflection of the seasons of life – love, loss, growth, and renewal – that we all walk through. Every word you've read holds a piece of my heart, written to inspire, uplift, and remind you that no matter where life leads, hope and togetherness light the path forward.

Stories have the power to connect us, to heal us, and to remind us that we are never truly alone. I encourage you to keep telling your stories – to write them, share them, and most importantly, live them. Life is precious, and every moment counts.

If my words have brought a smile, a memory, or a little bit of joy to your day, then I consider my mission fulfilled. I would love to hear from you, and your thoughts and reflections mean the world to me.

With heartfelt thanks,

Patricia A. Florio

Court Reporter, Author, and Storyteller

ABOUT THE AUTHOR

Patricia A. Florio is a passionate storyteller, advocate, and dedicated member of her community. With a background in journalism, Patricia's writing reflects her commitment to making meaningful connections and giving a voice to those who are often unheard.

Her books, including The Word Catcher, The Four Seasons, and Nick Alanzo, showcase her ability to weave compelling narratives that inspire, uplift, and empower. Through her work, Patricia shares her own journey of resilience, compassion, and an unwavering commitment to the power of words. Her writing continues to resonate with readers, offering valuable insights and reflections.

About the Book

The Four Seasons by Patricia A. Florio is a heartfelt journey through the rhythms of life, friendship, and love. Divided into four seasons—Spring, Summer, Fall, and Winter—each chapter of this memoir paints vivid snapshots of Patricia's life and the people who have shaped her journey.

From the chaos of moving into a new home in Ocean Grove to cherished moments with close friends, Patricia's narrative is rich with warmth, humor, and poignant reflection. Through personal anecdotes, including her relationships, family dynamics, and the ups and downs of life, *The Four Seasons* brings to life the spirit of change, growth, and deep connection. Whether navigating new beginnings or revisiting treasured memories, Patricia's story invites readers into a world where every season holds a lesson.

A beautiful meditation on time, relationships, and the unpredictable passage of life, *The Four Seasons* is for anyone who cherishes the beauty of life's transitions and the enduring power of friendship and love.

ABOUT THE PUBLISHER

At **America Publishers**, we believe every author has a unique voice that deserves to be heard. Dedicated to supporting storytellers across the globe, our mission is to bring quality books to life while empowering authors to share their messages with the world.

Our services range from manuscript editing and formatting to book design, publishing, and global distribution. With a team passionate about creativity and excellence, we ensure every book reflects the heart and soul of its author.

Why Choose America Publishers?

- Global Reach: Your book, distributed across major platforms like Amazon, Barnes & Noble, and more.

- Personalized Services: Tailored support to bring your vision to life.

- Proven Expertise: Helping hundreds of authors transform their manuscripts into published works.

To learn more about our work or inquire about publishing your own story, visit:

https://americapublishers.com

Follow us on social media for updates and author highlights:

Facebook: America Publishers

Instagram: @america_publishers_official

www.ingramcontent.com/pod-product-compliance
Lightning Source LLC
LaVergne TN
LVHW021715080426
835510LV00010B/1004